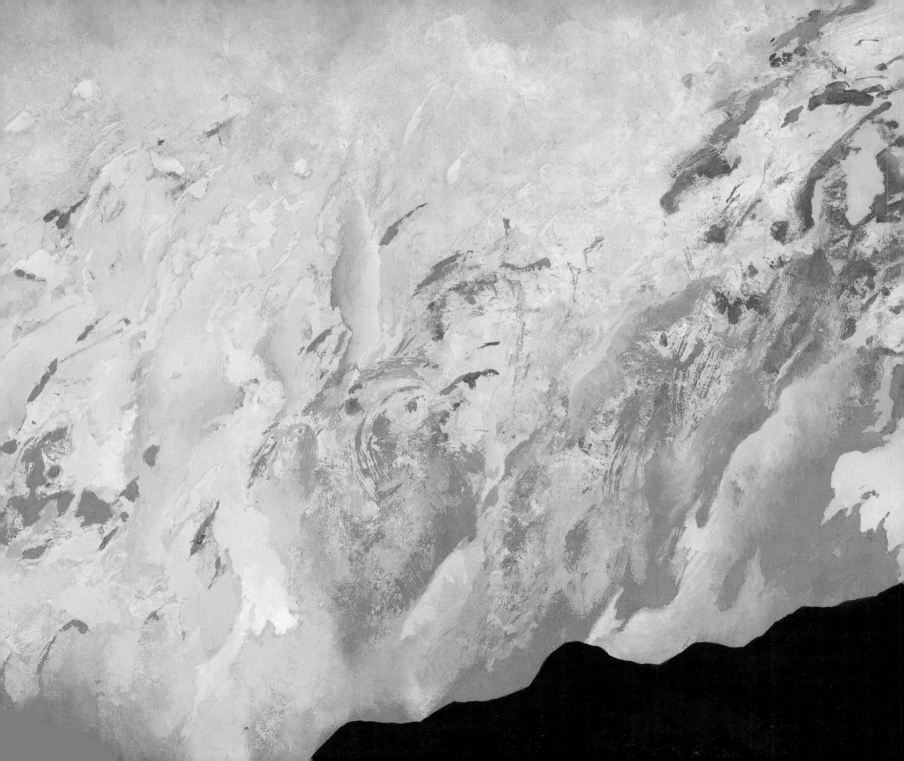

STAGE 2

Volcanoes

by **Franklyn M. Branley** • illustrated by **Megan Lloyd**

Collins
An Imprint of HarperCollinsPublishers

The Let's-Read-and-Find-Out Science book series was originated
by Dr. Franklyn M. Branley, Astronomer Emeritus and former Chairman of the
American Museum–Hayden Planetarium, and was formerly co-edited by him and Dr. Roma
Gans, Professor Emeritus of Childhood Education, Teachers College, Columbia University. Text
and illustrations for each of the books in the series are checked for accuracy by an expert
in the relevant field. For more information about Let's-Read-and-Find-Out Science
books, write to HarperCollins Children's Books, 1350 Avenue of the Americas,
New York, NY 10019, or visit our website at www.letsreadandfindout.com.

Let's-Read-and-Find-Out Science® is a trademark of HarperCollins Publishers.
Collins is an imprint of HarperCollins Publishers.
Volcanoes
Text copyright © 1985 by Franklyn M. Branley
Illustrations copyright © 2008 by Megan Lloyd

Library of Congress Cataloging-in-Publication Data
Branley, Franklyn Mansfield.
Volcanoes / by Franklyn M. Branley ; illustrated by Megan Lloyd.—Newly illustrated ed.
p.   cm. — (Let's-read-and-find-out science. Stage 2)
ISBN-10: 0-06-028011-5 (trade bdg.) — ISBN-13: 978-0-06-028011-6 (trade bdg.)
ISBN-10: 0-06-445189-5 (pbk. bdg.) — ISBN-13: 978-0-06-445189-5 (pbk. bdg.)
1. Volcanoes—Juvenile literature. I. Lloyd, Megan, ill. II. Title. III. Series.
QE521.3.B73 2008   2006000465
551.21—dc22

Typography by Rachel L. Schoenberg
1 2 3 4 5 6 7 8 9 10
❖
Newly Illustrated Edition, 2008

For Matthew the inquisitive!
—M.L.

Special thanks to Professor Bill Menke,
Lamont—Doherty Earth Observatory of Columbia
University, for his time and expert review.

In the year 79 Mount Vesuvius, a volcano in Italy, blew up.

Hot, melted rock from deep inside the earth pushed up through the mountain. The top of the mountain exploded. Ash, cinders and stones buried Pompeii, a great city below the mountain.

Nearly two thousand years later Mount Vesuvius still
spouts steam and ash. But not as much as it did long ago.
In 1815 the same thing happened in Indonesia, a group of
islands between Asia and Australia. Mount Tambora blew
its top. Billions of tons of the mountain were turned into
ash and thrown into the air. Winds carried the ash
all around the earth. It made a cloud that blocked
out the sun. The earth got colder and colder.
The next year, 1816, was called the year without
a summer. The New England states had six
inches of snow in June, and there
were frosts in July and August.
That's how cold it was.

JUNE 1816

In 1980, in the state of Washington, the top of Mount St. Helens blew up. Before it did, the earth shook. There was a rumble and bang so loud, it was heard 300 miles away.

When the mountain exploded, steam, gas and ash were thrown into the air. The top of the mountain was gone. It had turned into hot ash.

Lightning flashed inside the dark clouds.

Huge trees were flattened by the blast. Here and there the heat started fires. The hot ash melted snow on the mountain and made a thick mud that flowed down into the valleys. The mud covered fields and forests. Lakes, ponds and rivers were filled with it. The mud buried animals, houses and people.

The eruption of Mount St. Helens was not a surprise. Geologists, people who study the earth, knew that the volcano had erupted about a hundred years ago. And it was bound to happen again.

Geologists watch volcanoes for signs of an eruption. They listen for rumblings. Mount St. Helens had been rumbling off and on for more than a hundred years. Geologists knew that these rumblings were warnings.

Geologists also measure earthquakes. Before a volcano erupts, there are usually earthquakes in the region.

Volcanoes and earthquakes occur because our planet is always changing. Parts of it are always moving.

The earth is covered with soil, sand and broken rocks. Under that are layers of solid rock. The layers are broken into huge sections called plates. Geologists have given the plates names.

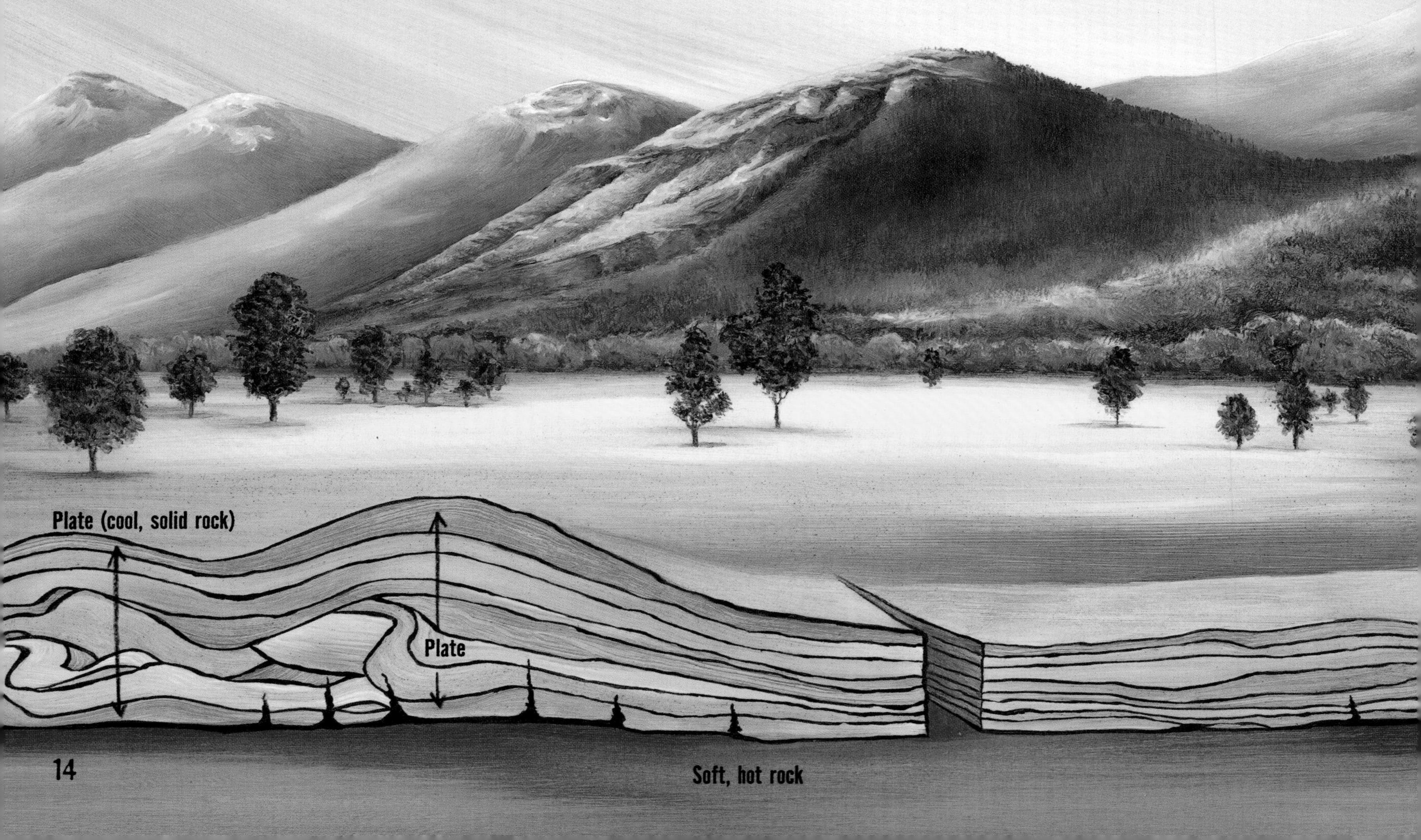

Plate (cool, solid rock)

Plate

Soft, hot rock

Under the plates there is very hot rock. The plates move on the hot rock, which is soft like dough. They don't move much, only about as fast as your fingernails grow. But they keep moving year after year after year. They have moved for millions of years.

Plate

Plate (cool, solid rock)

Soft, hot rock

Plate

Plate

Magma

In some places two plates move apart.
Where they do, hot, molten rock, called
magma, pushes up between them. After
it comes to the surface, magma is called
lava. The lava cools and becomes solid
rock. That is happening in places under
the oceans right now. Huge underwater
mountain ranges have been building up
for hundreds of millions of years.

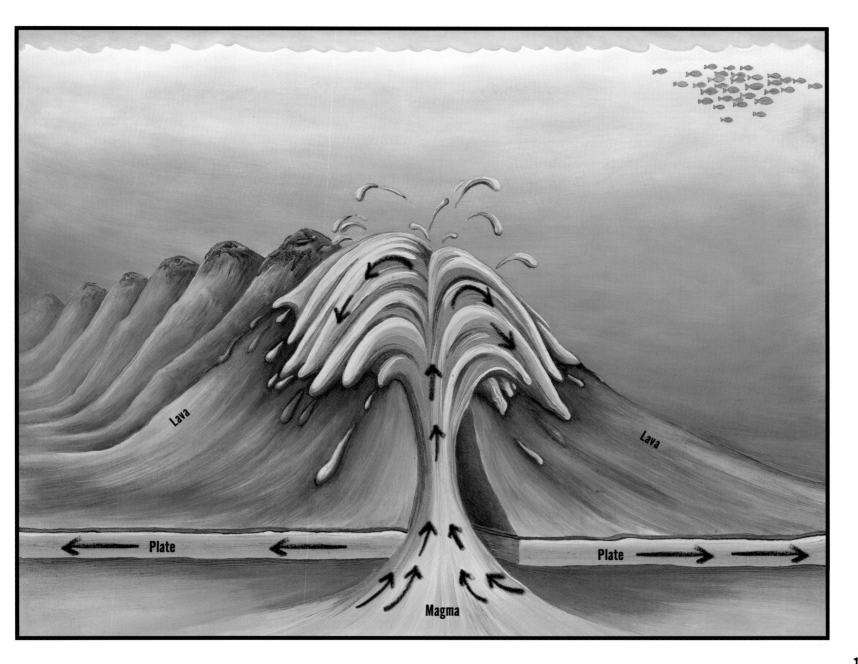

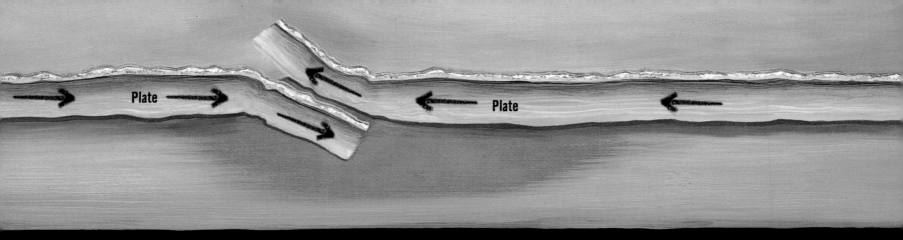

In some places plates move apart.
In other places they push together,
and one plate moves under another. Or
one plate may slide past another. These
movements shake the earth. They
make earthquakes.

At Mount St. Helens an edge of the small Juan de Fuca Plate has been moving under the North American Plate for thousands of years. As it has moved under, the heavy plates have rubbed together. The friction between the plates made the lower plate hot enough to melt. The hot, molten rock pushed upward. Most of the magma stayed under the mountain. It pushed upward but did not break through. Some came through cracks in the side of Mount St. Helens.

Heat, steam and pressure from the magma blew off the top of the mountain.

Mount St. Helens

Pacific Ocean

Juan de Fuca Plate

North American Plate

Magma

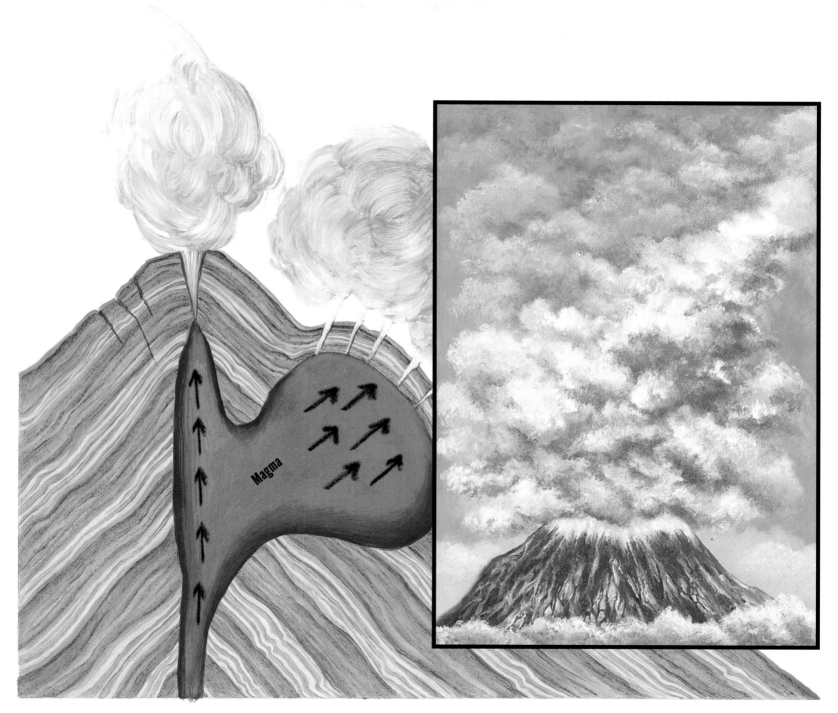

Magma

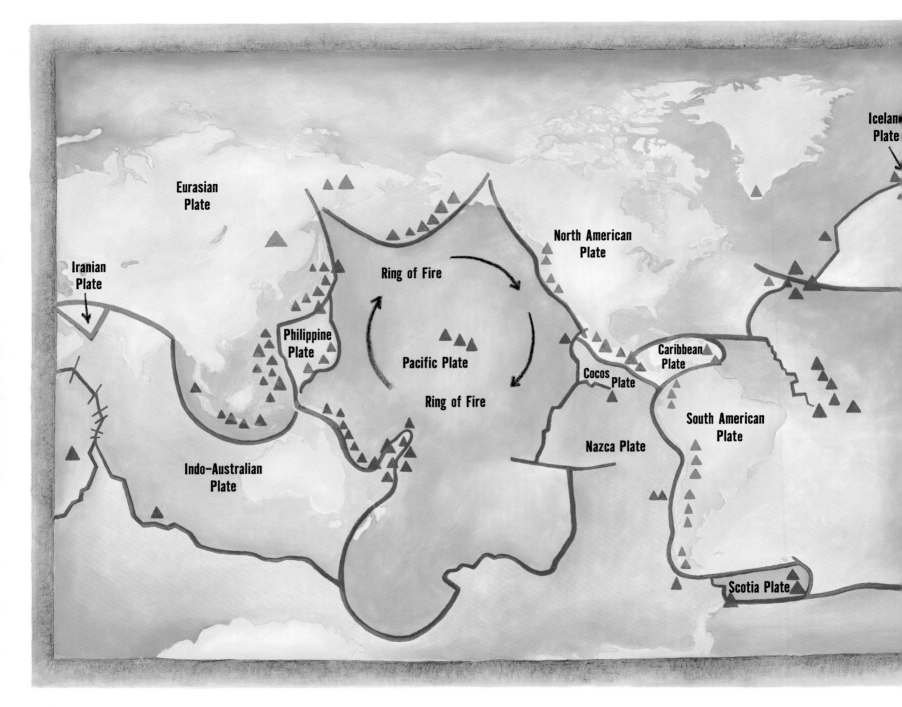

Eurasian
Plate

Iranian
Plate

Philippine
Plate

Ring of Fire

Pacific Plate

Ring of Fire

Indo-Australian
Plate

North American
Plate

Iceland
Plate

Cocos
Plate

Caribbean
Plate

Nazca Plate

South American
Plate

Scotia Plate

Eurasian Plate

Iranian Plate

Arabian Plate

ican ate

ate boundaries

Volcanoes don't happen just anywhere.

The map shows where volcanoes are located around the world. You can see that they usually occur where one plate meets another.

Most volcanoes are along the shores of the Pacific Ocean. They are at the edge of the huge Pacific Plate. There are so many that the region is called the Ring of Fire. That's also where most earthquakes occur.

Some volcanoes are not on plate edges. Hawaii is in the middle of the Pacific Plate. There molten rock pushes up through a weak spot in the plate. The islands of Hawaii are made from the lava that has built up.

As the islands have formed, they have been carried slowly northwest by the movement of the plate.

Volcanoes are still erupting on Hawaii. New lava is coming to the surface.

There are thousands of volcanoes around the world. Some erupted millions of years ago but will probably never erupt again. They are inactive. Others are active. They could go off again.

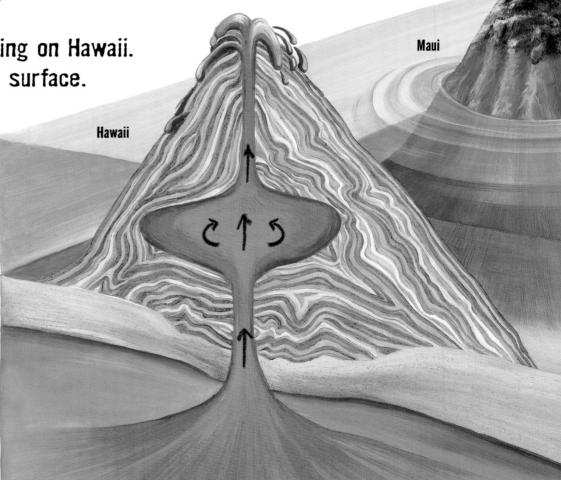

Hawaii

Maui

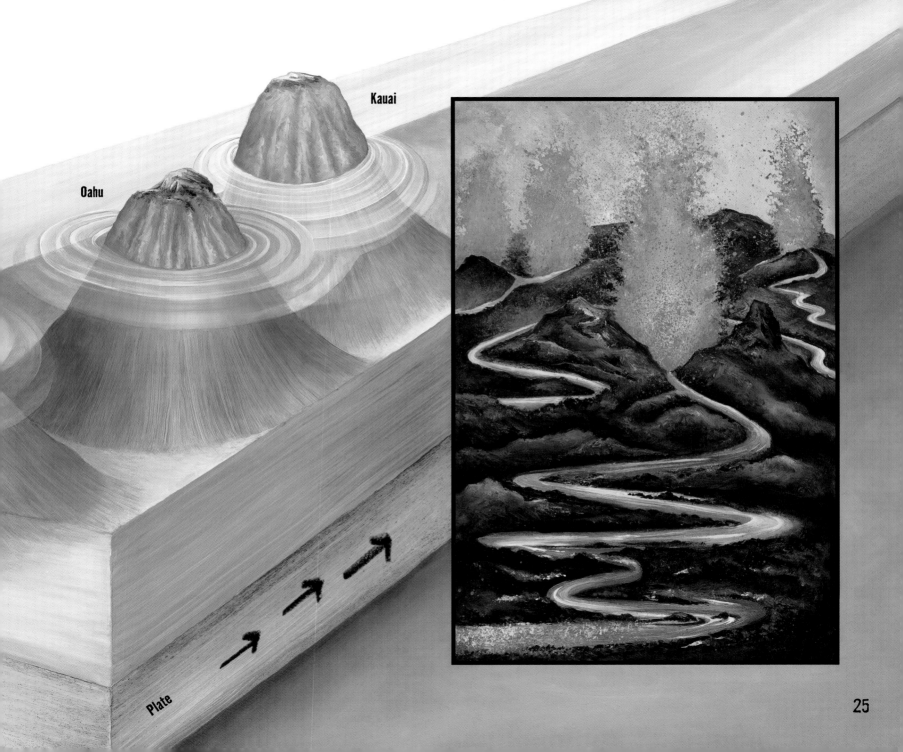

Oahu

Kauai

Plate

From time to time a new volcano will appear.

When a new volcano begins, the ground may get warmer. There may be small earthquakes, and steam may come out of the ground. That's what happened in 1943 at Parícutin in Mexico. Parícutin is on a boundary between two plates. One plate dug under another, and a field became a volcano.

The farmer who owned it, Dionisio Pulido, noticed his field was getting warmer. After a few days the field cracked open, and steam and molten rock spurted out of it. A bulge grew in the field, and it got higher and higher. The field became a hill and then a small mountain. The mountain became hotter and hotter. Rocks, steam, lava and ash were thrown out of cracks in it.

Ash covered the countryside. Winds carried the ash as far as 200 miles away. Houses and churches were covered. Whole towns were buried under ash. Dionisio Pulido's farm was gone. It had become a volcano nearly a quarter mile high.

Geologists cannot tell exactly when a new volcano will be born or when an old one will erupt. Small earthquakes or rumblings warn geologists that a volcano could erupt tomorrow. Then again, it might be months or even years before it happens.

Geologists do know that most volcanoes will occur along the Ring of Fire. If not there, the volcano will probably occur at the edge of some other plate.

But don't worry about a volcano in your backyard. That doesn't happen very often. Besides, geologists are always watching the earth for changes. Usually they are able to warn us long before a volcano blows its top.

Find Out More About Volcanoes

Volcano Facts

• Volcanoes are classified into three main types according to their eruption style and their shape. The three types are cinder cone, shield volcano and stratovolcano.

• The gases produced by volcanic eruptions millions of years ago constructed the current atmosphere on Earth.

• Some rock from the 1980 eruption of Mount St. Helens traveled as fast as 250 miles per hour.

• There are approximately 1,500 active volcanoes on the earth, and more than half of these volcanoes are located in the Ring of Fire.

• Volcanoes exist on planets other than the earth, including Venus and Mars. Our moon has several extinct volcanoes on its surface that are visible with a telescope. One of the most fascinating examples of volcanic activity is Jupiter's moon Io, which has volcanoes that are constantly erupting.

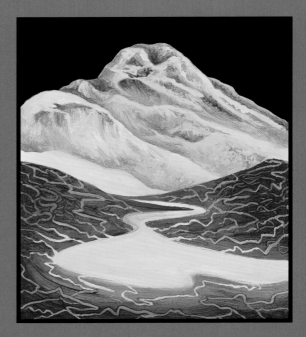

Erupting Volcano

You will need:

Cardboard box	An adult
Old newspapers	Eruption mixture:
Aluminum foil	1 cup of water
Wet sand	$3/4$ cup of vinegar
Empty soup can	$1/2$ cup of dishwashing liquid
$1/4$ cup of baking soda	10 drops of yellow food coloring
Large measuring cup	10 drops of red food coloring

Put the box on top of the old newspapers to protect your table's surface. Line your box with aluminum foil and fill the box with wet sand. Place the soup can in the center of the box. Form the sand around the can into a volcanic cone to complete your volcano. Make sure the can is completely hidden by the sand. Then pour the baking soda into the can. Measure out all the parts of the eruption mixture into one large measuring cup. To start the eruption, add the completed eruption mixture into the soup can and watch lava pour from your erupting volcano!